The Freedom of Forgiveness

Joshua Rhoades

Published by Joshua Paul Rhoades, 2024.

While every precaution has been taken in the preparation of this book, the publisher assumes no responsibility for errors or omissions, or for damages resulting from the use of the information contained herein.

THE FREEDOM OF FORGIVENESS

First edition. August 31, 2024.

ISBN: 979-8227267009

Written by Joshua Rhoades.

Also by Joshua Rhoades

Courage Under Fire: David's Stand On The Battlefield
Jonah's Journey: Voices Of Redemption And Lessons In Obedience
The Furnace Of Faith: 12 Principles From The Heat Of Faith
Whispers of Hope: Inspiring Stories of Men's Prayers In Scripture
Frontier Legends: The Oregon Dream
Elijah: A Beacon Of Boldness
HOOK, LINE & SAVIOUR - Faith Reflections from Fishing
Driven By Faith: Motor Racing Inspired Christian Life
30 Day Devotional - Bold and Strong- Coffee Devotions for a
Courageous Christian Walk
Authentic Christianity: The Heart of Old Time Religion
Consider The Ant - God's Tiny Preachers
Flee Fornication: The Plea For Purity
Renewed Hope- How to Find Encouragement in God
Sounding The Call - The Voice of Conviction
The Altar - Where Heaven Meets Earth
The Bible's Battlefields- Timeless Lessons from Ancient Wars
The Sacred Art of Silence - How Silence Speaks in Scripture
Under Fire- The Sanctity of the Traditional Biblical Home
Who Is on the Lord's Side? A Call to Righteousness
What Is Truth? - From Skepticism to Submission
First and Goal- Faith and Football Fundamentals
From Dugout to Devotion- Spiritual Lessons from Baseball
Par for the Course- Faith and Fairways
The Believer's Pace- Tools for Running Life's Marathon

Introduction

"The Freedom of Forgiveness" is a journey through one of the most powerful and transformative concepts in Scripture—an idea that has the capacity to heal wounds, restore relationships, and set souls free. Forgiveness is not merely a noble ideal; it is a divine mandate and a cornerstone of the Christian faith, one that is woven through the fabric of the Bible. In this book, we will explore the depth of forgiveness through the lives of individuals in Scripture who experienced its power firsthand, both in receiving and offering it.

Forgiveness is at the heart of the gospel message. From Genesis to Revelation, the Bible consistently shows us that the path to true freedom lies in the ability to forgive others and to accept the forgiveness offered by God. Through the stories of biblical figures, we see that forgiveness is not just an act but a process—a journey that requires courage, humility, and a deep reliance on God's grace.

One of the earliest and most profound examples of forgiveness is found in the story of Joseph. Betrayed by his own brothers, sold into slavery, and unjustly imprisoned, Joseph had every reason to harbor resentment and seek revenge. Yet, when he was finally in a position of power, Joseph chose a different path. In Genesis 50:20, he tells his brothers, "But as for you, ye thought evil against me; but God meant it unto good,". Joseph's ability to forgive not only brought healing to his family but also demonstrated the sovereignty of God in turning even the darkest situations into opportunities for grace.

Another powerful example is King David. Despite being a man after God's own heart, David committed grievous sins, including adultery and murder. When confronted by the prophet Nathan, David's response was one of deep repentance, captured in Psalm 51. David's story shows us that forgiveness is not only about forgiving others but also about seeking and accepting God's forgiveness when we fall short. David's life illustrates the freedom that comes when we confess our sins and allow God's grace to cleanse and restore us.

The New Testament also provides profound lessons on forgiveness, most notably in the parable of the prodigal son. In Luke 15, Jesus tells the story of a wayward son who, after squandering his inheritance, returns home expecting judgment but instead receives a warm embrace from his father. This parable illustrates God's boundless love and His readiness to forgive, no matter how far we have strayed. It is a vivid reminder that forgiveness is always available to those who seek it with a repentant heart.

Of course, the ultimate example of forgiveness is found in Jesus Christ Himself. On the cross, bearing the weight of humanity's sins, Jesus prayed for those who crucified Him, saying, "Father, forgive them; for they know not what they do" (Luke 23:34). This act of forgiveness, offered in the midst of unimaginable suffering, stands as the ultimate testament to the power of forgiveness and its ability to break the chains of sin and guilt.

"The Freedom of Forgiveness" invites you to reflect on these biblical examples and many others, encouraging you to embrace the transformative power of forgiveness in your own life. Whether you struggle to forgive someone who has wronged you, or you find it difficult to accept God's forgiveness for your own mistakes, this book offers hope and guidance. Through the stories of Scripture, you will discover that forgiveness is not just an obligation, but a pathway to freedom—a freedom that releases us from the burdens of the past and opens the door to a future filled with peace, reconciliation, and the fullness of God's grace.

Chapter 1 The Serenity Of Forgiveness

Joseph was one of Jacob's twelve sons, and his story is one of great trials and incredible forgiveness. His brothers, out of jealousy, sold him into slavery, which led him to Egypt. Despite being wronged, Joseph showed an amazing level of forgiveness, a trait that is so important in the Christian life. The Bible, specifically the King James Version, provides verses that help us understand the depth of Joseph's forgiveness and how we can apply it in our lives.

Joseph's story begins with his brothers' jealousy. Genesis 37:4 says, "And when his brethren saw that their father loved him more than all his brethren, they hated him, and could not speak peaceably unto him." This hatred led them to plot against him. Genesis 37:18-20 states, "And when they saw him afar off, even before he came near unto them, they conspired against him to slay him. And they said one to another, Behold, this dreamer cometh. Come now therefore, and let us slay him, and cast him into some pit, and we will say, Some evil beast hath devoured him: and we shall see what will become of his dreams." However, instead of killing him, they decided to sell him into slavery. Genesis 37:27-28 records, "Come, and let us sell him to the Ishmeelites, and let not our hand be upon him; for he is our brother and our flesh. And his brethren were content. Then there passed by Midianites merchantmen; and they drew and lifted up Joseph out of the pit, and sold Joseph to the Ishmeelites for twenty pieces of silver: and they brought Joseph into Egypt."

Joseph's life in Egypt was not easy. He was sold to Potiphar, an officer of Pharaoh. Genesis 39:1 states, "And Joseph was brought down to Egypt; and Potiphar, an officer of Pharaoh, captain of the guard, an Egyptian, bought him of the hands of the Ishmeelites, which had brought him down thither." Despite the hardships, Joseph prospered because of God's favor. Genesis 39:2-3 says, "And the LORD was with Joseph, and he was a prosperous man; and he was in the house of his master the Egyptian. And his master saw that the LORD was with him, and that the LORD made all that he did to prosper in his hand."

Joseph faced another trial when Potiphar's wife falsely accused him of trying to lie with her, resulting in his imprisonment. Genesis 39:19-20 recounts, "And it came to pass, when his master heard the words of his wife, which she spake unto him, saying, After this manner did thy servant to me; that his wrath was kindled. And Joseph's master took him, and put him into the prison, a place where the king's prisoners were bound: and he was there in the prison." Even in prison, Joseph found favor with the prison keeper. Genesis 39:21-22 tells us, "But the LORD was with Joseph, and shewed him mercy, and gave him favour in the sight of the keeper of the prison. And the keeper of the prison committed to Joseph's hand all the prisoners that were in the prison; and whatsoever they did there, he was the doer of it."

Joseph's ability to interpret dreams eventually led to his rise to power in Egypt. Genesis 41:14-16 says, "Then Pharaoh sent and called Joseph, and they brought him hastily out of the dungeon: and he shaved himself, and changed his raiment, and came in unto Pharaoh. And Pharaoh said unto Joseph, I have dreamed a dream, and there is none that can interpret it: and I have heard say of thee, that thou canst understand a dream to interpret it. And Joseph answered Pharaoh, saying, It is not in me: God shall give Pharaoh an answer of peace." Joseph interpreted Pharaoh's dreams, which predicted seven years of plenty followed by seven years of famine. Because of his wisdom, Pharaoh appointed Joseph as a ruler over Egypt. Genesis 41:39-41 records, "And Pharaoh said unto Joseph, Forasmuch as God hath shewed thee all this, there is none so discreet and wise as thou art: Thou shalt be over my house, and according unto thy word shall all my people be ruled: only in the throne will I be greater than thou. And Pharaoh said unto Joseph, See, I have set thee over all the land of Egypt."

When the famine came, Joseph's brothers came to Egypt to buy grain, not recognizing him. Genesis 42:6-8 states, "And Joseph was the governor over the land, and he it was that sold to all the people of the land: and Joseph's brethren came, and bowed down themselves before him with their faces to the earth. And Joseph saw his brethren, and he knew them, but made himself strange unto them, and spake roughly unto them; and he said unto them, Whence come ye? And they said, From the land of Canaan to buy food. And Joseph knew his brethren, but they knew not him." Despite having the power to take revenge, Joseph tested them to see if they had changed and eventually revealed himself to them. Genesis 45:3-5 tells us, "And Joseph said unto his brethren, I am Joseph; doth my father yet live? And his brethren could not answer him; for they were troubled at his presence. And Joseph said unto his brethren, Come near to me, I pray you. And they came near. And he said, I am Joseph your brother, whom ye sold into Egypt. Now therefore be not grieved, nor angry with yourselves, that ye sold me hither: for God did send me before you to preserve life."

Joseph's forgiveness was remarkable. He saw God's hand in his suffering and recognized that it was part of a greater plan. Genesis 50:19-21 captures this beautifully: "And Joseph said unto them, Fear not: for am I in the place of God? But as for you, ye thought evil against me; but God meant it unto good, to bring to pass, as it is this day, to save much people alive. Now therefore fear ye not: I will nourish you, and your little ones. And he comforted them, and spake kindly unto them." Joseph's attitude is a powerful lesson for Christians. He chose serenity and peace over bitterness and revenge. He allowed God to use his past hurts to bring about a greater good.

Christians today can learn a lot from Joseph's example. When family members or others wrong us, it can be difficult to forgive. However, we are called to forgive just as Joseph did. Matthew 6:14-15 says, "For if ye forgive men their trespasses, your heavenly Father will also forgive you: But if ye forgive not men their trespasses, neither will your Father forgive your trespasses." Forgiveness is not just a suggestion; it is a commandment. Ephesians 4:32 also emphasizes this: "And be ye kind one to another, tenderhearted, forgiving one another, even as God for Christ's sake hath forgiven you." Just as Joseph forgave his brothers, we too should seek to reconcile with those who have wronged us. This might mean letting go of past hurts and allowing God to heal our hearts.

Forgiving others can transform our lives and relationships. Colossians 3:13 instructs us, "Forbearing one another, and forgiving one another, if any man have a quarrel against any: even as Christ forgave you, so also do ye." This means bearing with each other and forgiving any grievances we may have against one another. It is through forgiveness that we can experience true peace and serenity. Philippians 4:7 promises, "And the peace of God, which passeth all understanding, shall keep your hearts and minds through Christ Jesus."

Moreover, forgiveness opens the door for God's blessings. Proverbs 28:13 states, "He that covereth his sins shall not prosper: but whoso confesseth and forsaketh them shall have mercy." By forgiving others and confessing our own sins, we invite God's mercy into our lives. Forgiveness also allows us to reflect God's love to others. 1 John 4:11 says, "Beloved, if God so loved us, we ought also to love one another." Our ability to forgive is a testament to the transformative power of God's love in our hearts.

Joseph's story teaches us that forgiveness is not just about letting go of anger, but also about trusting God's plan. Romans 8:28 reassures us, "And we know that all things work together for good to them that love God, to them who are the called according to his purpose." Even when we face betrayal or hardship, we can trust that God is working for our good. By forgiving others, we align ourselves with God's will and open ourselves up to His blessings.

In conclusion, Joseph's example of serenity and forgiveness is a powerful lesson for Christians. By forgiving family members and others who have wronged us, seeking reconciliation, and allowing God to turn past hurts into blessings, we can experience true peace and reflect God's love to the world. As we forgive, we fulfill God's commandments and invite His mercy and blessings into our lives. Let us strive to follow Joseph's example, trusting that God can use every situation for our good and His glory.

Chapter 2 The Surrender Of Forgiveness

Esau is a significant figure in the Bible, and his story teaches us about the importance of forgiveness and surrendering grudges. Esau was the elder brother of Jacob, and his story is found in the Book of Genesis. Esau's experience with his brother Jacob provides a profound lesson on letting go of past hurts and seeking reconciliation, even when deeply wronged. Esau was the firstborn son of Isaac and Rebekah, and as the firstborn, he was entitled to the birthright, which included the leadership of the family and a double portion of the inheritance. However, Esau lost his birthright and blessing to Jacob, his younger brother, in a series of events that caused deep hurt and anger.

In Genesis 25:29-34, we read about the moment when Esau sold his birthright to Jacob. Esau came from the field and was faint. He said to Jacob, "Feed me, I pray thee, with that same red pottage; for I am faint." Jacob took advantage of Esau's hunger and said, "Sell me this day thy birthright." Esau, driven by his immediate need, responded, "Behold, I am at the point to die: and what profit shall this birthright do to me?" Jacob then made Esau swear to sell him the birthright, and Esau sold his birthright to Jacob. This moment marked the beginning of Esau's loss and the start of his bitterness toward Jacob.

The deception continued when Isaac, their father, was old and his eyesight had dimmed. In Genesis 27:1-4, Isaac asked Esau to hunt and prepare a savory meal so that he could bless him before he died. Rebekah, their mother, overheard this and instructed Jacob to deceive Isaac by pretending to be Esau. Jacob did as his mother instructed, wearing Esau's clothes and using goat skins to mimic Esau's hairy skin. Isaac, unable to see clearly, blessed Jacob, thinking he was Esau. Genesis 27:27-29 records Isaac's blessing to Jacob, where he said, "Therefore God give thee of the dew of heaven, and the fatness of the earth, and plenty of corn and wine: Let people serve thee, and nations bow down to thee: be lord over thy brethren, and let thy mother's sons bow down to thee: cursed be every one that curseth thee, and blessed be he that blesseth thee."

When Esau returned and discovered what had happened, he was devastated. Genesis 27:34 says, "And when Esau heard the words of his father, he cried with a great and exceeding bitter cry, and said unto his father, Bless me, even me also, O my father." Isaac told Esau that Jacob had deceitfully taken his blessing, and Esau wept and begged for a blessing of his own. Isaac's response in Genesis 27:37-40 reveals the limited blessing Esau received compared to Jacob's: "And Isaac answered and said unto Esau, Behold, I have made him thy lord, and all his brethren have I given to him for servants; and with corn and wine have I sustained him: and what shall I do now unto thee, my son? And Esau said unto his father, Hast thou but one blessing, my father? bless me, even me also, O my father. And Esau lifted up his voice, and wept."

Esau's anger and desire for revenge are evident in Genesis 27:41, where it says, "And Esau hated Jacob because of the blessing wherewith his father blessed him: and Esau said in his heart, The days of mourning for my father are at hand; then will I slay my brother Jacob." Rebekah, hearing of Esau's plan, warned Jacob, and he fled to his uncle Laban's house. Years passed, and Jacob prospered, but the fear of meeting Esau again lingered. In Genesis 32, Jacob prepared to meet Esau, sending gifts ahead to appease his brother, fearing that Esau still held a grudge.

However, when the moment of reconciliation came, Esau demonstrated remarkable forgiveness and surrender. In Genesis 33:4, we read, "And Esau ran to meet him, and embraced him, and fell on his neck, and kissed him: and they wept." Instead of harboring bitterness, Esau chose to forgive Jacob and reconcile with him. This act of forgiveness is a powerful example for us. Esau's willingness to let go of his grudge and mend his relationship with Jacob shows the strength of his character and the importance of forgiveness in healing broken relationships.

As Christians, we are called to forgive those who have wronged us, just as Esau forgave Jacob. Holding onto grudges only leads to more pain and division. Ephesians 4:31-32 instructs us, "Let all bitterness, and wrath, and anger, and clamour, and evil speaking, be put away from you, with all malice: And be ye kind one to another, tenderhearted, forgiving one another, even as God for Christ's sake hath forgiven you." Esau's story teaches us to surrender our anger and bitterness, to embrace the opportunity for a fresh start, and to seek reconciliation with those who have hurt us.

Forgiving others is not always easy, especially when the wounds are deep. But Jesus taught us the importance of forgiveness in Matthew 6:14-15: "For if ye forgive men their trespasses, your heavenly Father will also forgive you: But if ye forgive not men their trespasses, neither will your Father forgive your trespasses." Forgiveness is not just about freeing the person who hurt us; it is also about freeing ourselves from the burden of anger and resentment.

Esau's act of forgiveness also reminds us of the transformative power of letting go. In Genesis 33:9, when Jacob offered Esau gifts to find favor in his sight, Esau replied, "I have enough, my brother; keep that thou hast unto thyself." Esau's contentment and his ability to move past his grievances reflect a heart that has truly surrendered to peace. Similarly, when we let go of grudges, we open ourselves up to the peace that surpasses all understanding, as promised in Philippians 4:7: "And the peace of God, which passeth all understanding, shall keep your hearts and minds through Christ Jesus."

In addition to the personal peace that comes from forgiveness, there is also the joy of restored relationships. Proverbs 17:9 says, "He that covereth a transgression seeketh love; but he that repeateth a matter separateth very friends." By forgiving Jacob, Esau sought love and reconciliation, mending the rift that had separated them for years. We too can seek to restore our relationships by covering transgression's with love and forgiveness.

The Bible encourages us to forgive repeatedly, just as God forgives us. In Matthew 18:21-22, Peter asked Jesus, "Lord, how oft shall my brother sin against me, and I forgive him? till seven times?" Jesus answered, "I say not unto thee, Until seven times: but, Until seventy times seven." This teaching emphasizes that forgiveness should be a continuous practice, not limited by the number of times we have been wronged.

Esau's forgiveness of Jacob is a testament to the power of surrendering grudges and choosing to forgive. It is a reminder that reconciliation is possible, even in the most strained relationships. Romans 12:18 advises us, "If it be possible, as much as lieth in you, live peaceably with all men." Striving for peace and reconciliation should be our goal as Christians, following Esau's example.

Forgiveness is a reflection of God's love and mercy. Colossians 3:13 tells us, "Forbearing one another, and forgiving one another, if any man have a quarrel against any: even as Christ forgave you, so also do ye." Just as Christ forgave us, we are called to forgive others. Esau's story shows us that forgiveness is not just a one-time act but a way of life that brings healing and restoration.

In conclusion, Esau's story of forgiveness and surrender teaches us valuable lessons about letting go of grudges and seeking reconciliation. By forgiving Jacob for stealing his birthright and blessing, Esau demonstrated the power of forgiveness to heal and restore relationships. As Christians, we are called to follow his example, embracing the opportunity for a fresh start and allowing God's peace to fill our hearts. Through forgiveness, we reflect God's love and mercy, bringing healing to ourselves and those around us. Let us strive to forgive, as Esau did, and experience the transformative power of surrendering our grudges and embracing reconciliation.

Chapter 3 The Supplication Of Forgiveness

Moses is a key figure in the Bible who teaches us the importance of supplication, especially when it comes to interceding for others. His story, particularly the part where he interceded for the Israelites after they made the golden calf, provides a powerful example of praying for those who have wronged us or others. In the book of Exodus, we find the Israelites, led by Moses, delivered from Egypt. They were on their way to the Promised Land when Moses went up Mount Sinai to receive the Ten Commandments from God. During this time, the people grew impatient and asked Aaron to make them gods to lead them. Exodus 32:1-4 recounts, "And when the people saw that Moses delayed to come down out of the mount, the people gathered themselves together unto Aaron, and said unto him, Up, make us gods, which shall go before us; for as for this Moses, the man that brought us up out of the land of Egypt, we wot not what is become of him. And Aaron said unto them, Break off the golden earrings, which are in the ears of your wives, of your sons, and of your daughters, and bring them unto me. And all the people brake off the golden earrings which were in their ears, and brought them unto Aaron. And he received them at their hand, and fashioned it with a graving tool, after he had made it a molten calf: and they said, These be thy gods, O Israel, which brought thee up out of the land of Egypt."

This act of creating and worshiping the golden calf was a great sin against God, who had just delivered them from slavery. God's response was one of anger. Exodus 32:7-10 describes, "And the LORD said unto Moses, Go, get thee down; for thy people, which thou broughtest out of the land of Egypt, have corrupted themselves: They have turned aside quickly out of the way which I commanded them: they have made them a molten calf, and have worshipped it, and have sacrificed thereunto, and said, These be thy gods, O Israel, which have brought thee up out of the land of Egypt. And the LORD said unto Moses, I have seen this people, and, behold, it is a stiffnecked people: Now therefore let me alone, that my wrath may wax hot against them, and that I may consume them: and I will make of thee a great nation."

In response, Moses demonstrated the power of supplication. He pleaded with God to forgive the Israelites and to remember His promises to Abraham, Isaac, and Israel. Exodus 32:11-14 records Moses' intercession, "And Moses besought the LORD his God, and said, LORD, why doth thy wrath wax hot against thy people, which thou hast brought forth out of the land of Egypt with great power, and with a mighty hand? Wherefore should the Egyptians speak, and say, For mischief did he bring them out, to slay them in the mountains, and to consume them from the face of the earth? Turn from thy fierce wrath, and repent of this evil against thy people. Remember Abraham, Isaac, and Israel, thy servants, to whom thou swarest by thine own self, and saidst unto them, I will multiply your seed as the stars of heaven, and all this land that I have spoken of will I give unto your seed, and they shall inherit it for ever. And the LORD repented of the evil which he thought to do unto his people."

Moses' prayer was effective because it was rooted in God's promises and character. He appealed to God's mercy and faithfulness, reminding God of His covenant with the patriarchs. This kind of prayer, where one intercedes for others, asking God to forgive and help them change, is a powerful tool for Christians today. Moses' supplication didn't just end there. When he came down from the mountain and saw the people worshiping the calf, he was so angry that he broke the tablets of the commandments. He took the calf, burned it, ground it to powder, scattered it on the water, and made the Israelites drink it (Exodus 32:19-20). Despite his anger, Moses' concern was for the people's spiritual well-being. He knew their sin had serious consequences, and he sought to make atonement for them.

In Exodus 32:30-32, Moses again interceded for the people: "And it came to pass on the morrow, that Moses said unto the people, Ye have sinned a great sin: and now I will go up unto the LORD; peradventure I shall make an atonement for your sin. And Moses returned unto the LORD, and said, Oh, this people have sinned a great sin, and have made them gods of gold. Yet now, if thou wilt forgive their sin; and if not, blot me, I pray thee, out of thy book which thou hast written." This shows the depth of Moses' love and commitment to his people. He was willing to sacrifice himself for their forgiveness.

God's response in Exodus 32:33-34 was merciful yet just: "And the LORD said unto Moses, Whosoever hath sinned against me, him will I blot out of my book. Therefore now go, lead the people unto the place of which I have spoken unto thee: behold, mine Angel shall go before thee: nevertheless in the day when I visit I will visit their sin upon them." God forgave the people, but there were still consequences for their actions.

This story of Moses' supplication teaches us the importance of intercessory prayer. When others wrong us or sin against God, we should pray for them, asking God to forgive and change their hearts. James 5:16 encourages us to pray for one another: "Confess your faults one to another, and pray one for another, that ye may be healed. The effectual fervent prayer of a righteous man availeth much."

Jesus also emphasized the power of intercessory prayer. In Matthew 5:44, He taught, "But I say unto you, Love your enemies, bless them that curse you, do good to them that hate you, and pray for them which despitefully use you, and persecute you." Praying for those who have wronged us is an expression of love and obedience to God. It reflects the heart of Christ, who prayed for His persecutors even while on the cross. Luke 23:34 records His prayer: "Then said Jesus, Father, forgive them; for they know not what they do. And they parted his raiment, and cast lots."

Moses' example of supplication also reminds us to stand in the gap for others, especially when they have strayed from God's path. Ezekiel 22:30 highlights the importance of intercessors: "And I sought for a man among them, that should make up the hedge, and stand in the gap before me for the land, that I should not destroy it: but I found none." As Christians, we are called to stand in the gap through prayer, asking God to show mercy and guide people back to Him.

Intercessory prayer requires humility and a genuine concern for others. Philippians 2:4 instructs us, "Look not every man on his own things, but every man also on the things of others." By praying for others, we demonstrate love and compassion, fulfilling the law of Christ. Galatians 6:2 says, "Bear ye one another's burdens, and so fulfil the law of Christ."

Moses' prayers were rooted in his relationship with God. He spoke to God as a friend, and his intimacy with God made his intercession powerful. Exodus 33:11 describes their relationship: "And the LORD spake unto Moses face to face, as a man speaketh unto his friend." Our prayers, too, become powerful when we cultivate a close relationship with God, seeking His will and trusting in His promises.

In conclusion, Moses' example of supplication after the Israelites made the golden calf teaches us the importance of interceding for others. By praying for those who have wronged us or others, asking God to forgive them and help them change their ways, we reflect God's love and mercy. Intercessory prayer is a powerful tool that can bring about healing and reconciliation. Let us follow Moses' example, standing in the gap and lifting others up in prayer, trusting in God's faithfulness and grace. Through supplication, we can make a difference in the lives of those around us and fulfill our calling as intercessors.

Chapter 4 The Safeguard Of Forgiveness

David is one of the most significant figures in the Bible, known for his courage, faith, and, importantly, his mercy. His relationship with King Saul provides a powerful example of how to show mercy to those who seek to harm us and trust in God's justice rather than seeking revenge. The story of David and Saul is found in the books of 1 Samuel and 2 Samuel. David was chosen by God to be the next king of Israel after Saul, but Saul became jealous of David's success and popularity. Despite Saul's attempts to kill him, David repeatedly showed mercy and trusted God to deliver justice.

The story begins with David's rise to prominence after he defeated Goliath. In 1 Samuel 17:50, we read, "So David prevailed over the Philistine with a sling and with a stone, and smote the Philistine, and slew him; but there was no sword in the hand of David." This victory brought David into the favor of King Saul initially, but as David continued to succeed in battle, Saul's jealousy grew. In 1 Samuel 18:7-9, the women sang, "Saul hath slain his thousands, and David his ten thousands. And Saul was very wroth, and the saying displeased him; and he said, They have ascribed unto David ten thousands, and to me they have ascribed but thousands: and what can he have more but the kingdom? And Saul eyed David from that day and forward."

Saul's jealousy turned into a deadly pursuit. In 1 Samuel 19:1, "And Saul spake to Jonathan his son, and to all his servants, that they should kill David." David fled from Saul and spent years on the run, often narrowly escaping Saul's attempts to capture and kill him. Despite these threats, David never retaliated or sought revenge. One of the most significant moments demonstrating David's mercy occurred in the wilderness of En-gedi. Saul entered a cave to rest, not knowing David and his men were hiding there. David's men saw this as an opportunity to kill

Saul and end their troubles. But David refused. In 1 Samuel 24:4-7, "And the men of David said unto him, Behold the day of which the LORD said unto thee, Behold, I will deliver thine enemy into thine hand, that thou mayest do to him as it shall seem good unto thee. Then David arose, and cut off the skirt of Saul's robe privily. And it came to pass afterward, that David's heart smote him, because he had cut off Saul's skirt. And he said unto his men, The LORD forbid that I should do this thing unto my master, the LORD'S anointed, to stretch forth mine hand against him, seeing he is the anointed of the LORD. So David stayed his servants with these words, and suffered them not to rise against Saul."

David spared Saul's life and later confronted him, showing the piece of Saul's robe to prove he meant no harm. In 1 Samuel 24:10-12, David said, "Behold, this day thine eyes have seen how that the LORD had delivered thee to day into mine hand in the cave: and some bade me kill thee: but mine eye spared thee; and I said, I will not put forth mine hand against my lord; for he is the LORD'S anointed. Moreover, my father, see, yea, see the skirt of thy robe in my hand: for in that I cut off the skirt of thy robe, and killed thee not, know thou and see that there is neither evil nor transgression in mine hand, and I have not sinned against thee; yet thou huntest my soul to take it. The LORD judge between me and thee, and the LORD avenge me of thee: but mine hand shall not be upon thee." David's actions showed his deep respect for God's anointed king and his trust in God's justice.

Saul was moved by David's mercy. In 1 Samuel 24:16-19, "And it came to pass, when David had made an end of speaking these words unto Saul, that Saul said, Is this thy voice, my son David? And Saul lifted up his voice, and wept. And he said to David, Thou art more righteous than I: for thou hast rewarded me good, whereas I have rewarded thee evil. And thou hast shewed this day how that thou hast dealt well with me: forasmuch as when the LORD had delivered me into thine hand, thou killedst me not. For if a man find his enemy, will he let him go well away?

wherefore the LORD reward thee good for that thou hast done unto me this day."

David had another opportunity to kill Saul in 1 Samuel 26. Saul and his men were sleeping in their camp, and David and Abishai snuck in. Abishai wanted to kill Saul, but David again refused. In 1 Samuel 26:9-11, "And David said to Abishai, Destroy him not: for who can stretch forth his hand against the LORD'S anointed, and be guiltless? David said furthermore, As the LORD liveth, the LORD shall smite him; or his day shall come to die; or he shall descend into battle, and perish. The LORD forbid that I should stretch forth mine hand against the LORD'S anointed: but, I pray thee, take thou now the spear that is at his bolster, and the cruse of water, and let us go." David took Saul's spear and water jug to show he had been there but had spared Saul's life once more.

When David confronted Saul again, Saul acknowledged his sin and recognized David's righteousness. In 1 Samuel 26:21-24, "Then said Saul, I have sinned: return, my son David: for I will no more do thee harm, because my soul was precious in thine eyes this day: behold, I have played the fool, and have erred exceedingly. And David answered and said, Behold the king's spear! and let one of the young men come over and fetch it. The LORD render to every man his righteousness and his faithfulness: for the LORD delivered thee into my hand to day, but I would not stretch forth mine hand against the LORD'S anointed. And, behold, as thy life was much set by this day in mine eyes, so let my life be much set by in the eyes of the LORD, and let him deliver me out of all tribulation."

David's mercy and trust in God's justice stand as powerful lessons for us. He showed mercy to someone who actively sought to harm him, choosing to trust God rather than taking matters into his own hands. This aligns with the teachings of Jesus in the New Testament. In Matthew 5:7, Jesus said, "Blessed are the merciful: for they shall obtain mercy." By showing mercy, we reflect God's character and receive His mercy in return. Furthermore, David's actions demonstrate his trust in God's justice. Romans 12:19 advises, "Dearly beloved, avenge not yourselves, but rather give place unto wrath: for it is written, Vengeance is mine; I will repay, saith the Lord." David trusted that God would deal with Saul in His own time and way, a principle we are called to follow. When wronged, we should refrain from seeking revenge and instead leave justice to God, who judges righteously.

David's example also underscores the importance of respecting God's authority and those He appoints. Despite Saul's actions, David honored him as the LORD's anointed. This respect for God's chosen leader is reflected in 1 Peter 2:17, "Honour all men. Love the brotherhood. Fear God. Honour the king." Even when leaders fail, we are called to respect and pray for them, trusting God's sovereignty over all authorities.

Moreover, David's story encourages us to respond to hatred with goodness. Proverbs 25:21-22 says, "If thine enemy be hungry, give him bread to eat; and if he be thirsty, give him water to drink: For thou shalt heap coals of fire upon his head, and the LORD shall reward thee." By sparing Saul and treating him with kindness, David heaped coals of fire on Saul's head, leading Saul to recognize his own wrongdoing.

David's mercy extended beyond Saul to others who wronged him. When Absalom, David's son, rebelled against him, David instructed his commanders to deal gently with Absalom for his sake (2 Samuel 18:5). Even though Absalom sought to overthrow him, David's love and mercy for his son remained. When Absalom was killed, David mourned deeply, showing his compassionate heart (2 Samuel 18:33).

David's attitude of mercy and trust in God's justice can inspire us to respond similarly when we face conflicts or are wronged. Colossians 3:12-13 urges us, "Put on therefore, as the elect of God, holy and beloved, bowels of mercies, kindness, humbleness of mind, meekness, longsuffering; Forbearing one another, and forgiving one another, if any man have a quarrel against any: even as Christ forgave you, so also do ye." By showing mercy and forgiving others, we reflect the grace and forgiveness we have received from Christ.

In conclusion, David's story of mercy towards King Saul provides a powerful example of how to handle those who seek to harm us. He chose to show mercy and trust in God's justice rather than seeking revenge. This aligns with biblical teachings to be merciful, leave vengeance to God, respect authority, and respond to hatred with kindness. By following David's example, we can navigate conflicts with a heart of mercy, trusting in God's perfect justice and reflecting His love to those around us. Let us strive to embody these principles in our lives, knowing that God honors and rewards those who show mercy and trust in Him.

Chapter 5 The Sacrifice Of Forgiveness

Stephen is a remarkable figure in the Bible whose story is found in the Book of Acts. He is known for his ultimate sacrifice and his powerful example of forgiveness. Stephen was one of the first deacons in the early Christian church, chosen because he was "full of faith and of the Holy Ghost" (Acts 6:5). His story, particularly his martyrdom, teaches us about sacrifice and forgiveness, even in the face of severe persecution. Stephen was a man of great faith who performed miracles and spoke with wisdom. Acts 6:8 says, "And Stephen, full of faith and power, did great wonders and miracles among the people." However, his boldness in preaching the Gospel led to opposition from certain members of the synagogue. They couldn't resist the wisdom and spirit by which he spoke, so they stirred up the people and falsely accused him of blasphemy. Acts 6:12-14 describes the situation: "And they stirred up the people, and the elders, and the scribes, and came upon him, and caught him, and brought him to the council, And set up false witnesses, which said, This man ceaseth not to speak blasphemous words against this holy place, and the law: For we have heard him say, that this Jesus of Nazareth shall destroy this place, and shall change the customs which Moses delivered us."

Despite the false accusations, Stephen remained calm and gave a powerful speech before the Sanhedrin, recounting the history of Israel and accusing the Jewish leaders of resisting the Holy Spirit and betraying and murdering the Righteous One, Jesus Christ. Acts 7:51-53 records his bold words: "Ye stiffnecked and uncircumcised in heart and ears, ye do always resist the Holy Ghost: as your fathers did, so do ye. Which of the prophets have not your fathers persecuted? and they have slain them which shewed before of the coming of the Just One; of whom ye have been now the betrayers and murderers: Who have received the law by the disposition of angels, and have not kept it."

Stephen's words cut to the heart, and the council members were furious. Acts 7:54 says, "When they heard these things, they were cut to the heart, and they gnashed on him with their teeth." But Stephen, full of the Holy Spirit, looked up to heaven and saw the glory of God, and Jesus standing at the right hand of God. Acts 7:55-56 describes this divine vision: "But he, being full of the Holy Ghost, looked up stedfastly into heaven, and saw the glory of God, and Jesus standing on the right hand of God, And said, Behold, I see the heavens opened, and the Son of man standing on the right hand of God."

This vision of Jesus gave Stephen the strength and peace to face what was coming next. The enraged council members dragged him out of the city and began to stone him. Even as he was being brutally killed, Stephen's focus was on Jesus, and he displayed incredible forgiveness. Acts 7:59-60 recounts his final moments: "And they stoned Stephen, calling upon God, and saying, Lord Jesus, receive my spirit. And he kneeled down, and cried with a loud voice, Lord, lay not this sin to their charge. And when he had said this, he fell asleep."

Stephen's last words are a powerful example of forgiveness. He prayed for his persecutors, asking God not to hold this sin against them. This mirrors Jesus' own words on the cross when He prayed for those who crucified Him. Luke 23:34 says, "Then said Jesus, Father, forgive them; for they know not what they do. And they parted his raiment, and cast lots." Stephen followed in Jesus' footsteps, showing that even in the face of death, we are called to forgive those who persecute us and pray for their salvation.

As Christians, we may not face the same extreme persecution that Stephen did, but we will encounter unfair treatment and opposition because of our faith. In these moments, we are called to respond with the same grace and forgiveness that Stephen demonstrated. Matthew 5:44 teaches us, "But I say unto you, Love your enemies, bless them that curse you, do good to them that hate you, and pray for them which despitefully use you, and persecute you." This command to love and pray for our enemies is challenging, but it reflects the heart of God and the example of Christ.

Stephen's story also reminds us of the importance of standing firm in our faith, even in the face of severe opposition. Ephesians 6:13 encourages us, "Wherefore take unto you the whole armour of God, that ye may be able to withstand in the evil day, and having done all, to stand." Stephen stood firm in his faith, boldly proclaiming the truth of the Gospel, even though it cost him his life. His courage and faithfulness inspire us to be steadfast in our own walk with God.

Furthermore, Stephen's vision of Jesus standing at the right hand of God gives us hope and assurance that Jesus is with us in our trials. Hebrews 12:2 urges us to look to Jesus, "Looking unto Jesus the author and finisher of our faith; who for the joy that was set before him endured the cross, despising the shame, and is set down at the right hand of the throne of God." Stephen kept his eyes on Jesus, and this gave him the strength to forgive his persecutors and face death with peace.

Stephen's martyrdom also had a significant impact on the early church. Acts 8:1-4 describes how the church was scattered because of the persecution that arose after Stephen's death, but those who were scattered "went every where preaching the word." Stephen's sacrifice helped spread the Gospel even further, showing that God can bring good out of even the most difficult situations. Romans 8:28 reminds us, "And we know that all things work together for good to them that love God, to them who are the called according to his purpose."

In moments of persecution or unfair treatment, it is natural to feel anger and desire revenge. But as followers of Christ, we are called to a higher standard. Romans 12:17-21 instructs us, "Recompense to no man evil for evil. Provide things honest in the sight of all men. If it be possible, as much as lieth in you, live peaceably with all men. Dearly beloved, avenge not yourselves, but rather give place unto wrath: for it is written, Vengeance is mine; I will repay, saith the Lord. Therefore if thine enemy hunger, feed him; if he thirst, give him drink: for in so doing thou shalt heap coals of fire on his head. Be not overcome of evil, but overcome evil with good." By forgiving our persecutors and praying for their salvation, we overcome evil with good and reflect the character of Christ.

Stephen's example teaches us that forgiveness is not a sign of weakness but of strength and faith in God's justice. Psalm 37:5-6 encourages us, "Commit thy way unto the LORD; trust also in him; and he shall bring it to pass. And he shall bring forth thy righteousness as the light, and thy judgment as the noonday." When we forgive those who wrong us, we trust God to bring justice and vindicate us in His time.

In addition to forgiving our persecutors, we are also called to pray for their salvation. 1 Timothy 2:1-4 says, "I exhort therefore, that, first of all, supplications, prayers, intercessions, and giving of thanks, be made for all men; For kings, and for all that are in authority; that we may lead a quiet and peaceable life in all godliness and honesty. For this is good and acceptable in the sight of God our Saviour; Who will have all men to be saved, and to come unto the knowledge of the truth." Our prayers for our enemies can make a significant impact, as we ask God to open their hearts to the truth of the Gospel and transform their lives.

Stephen's story challenges us to examine our own hearts and attitudes towards those who wrong us. Colossians 3:12-13 instructs us, "Put on therefore, as the elect of God, holy and beloved, bowels of mercies, kindness, humbleness of mind, meekness, longsuffering; Forbearing one another, and forgiving one another, if any man have a quarrel against any: even as Christ forgave you, so also do ye." By cultivating a heart of mercy, kindness, and forgiveness, we become more like Christ and demonstrate His love to the world.

In conclusion, Stephen's example of sacrifice and forgiveness is a powerful lesson for us. Even in the face of death, he forgave those who were stoning him and prayed for their salvation. As Christians, we are called to respond to persecution and unfair treatment with the same grace and forgiveness, asking God to forgive our persecutors and praying for their salvation. By following Stephen's example, we reflect the heart of Christ, stand firm in our faith, and trust in God's justice. Let us strive to embody these principles in our lives, showing mercy, forgiving others, and praying for their salvation, knowing that God can bring good out of even the most difficult situations. Stephen's story reminds us that forgiveness is a powerful act of faith and love, and it can have a profound impact on our lives and the lives of those around us.

Chapter 6 The Second Chance Of Forgiveness

Peter is one of the most well-known disciples of Jesus, and his life is a powerful example of forgiveness and offering second chances. After Jesus' resurrection, Peter, who had denied Jesus three times, became a key leader in the early church. One of the most notable moments in Peter's ministry was when he forgave the Jews who had crucified Jesus and offered them the message of repentance and hope in Christ. This story is a profound example of extending forgiveness and sharing the message of salvation, even with those who have rejected or mocked our faith.

The story begins in the Book of Acts, where Peter and the other disciples received the Holy Spirit on the day of Pentecost. Acts 2:1-4 says, "And when the day of Pentecost was fully come, they were all with one accord in one place. And suddenly there came a sound from heaven as of a rushing mighty wind, and it filled all the house where they were sitting. And there appeared unto them cloven tongues like as of fire, and it sat upon each of them. And they were all filled with the Holy Ghost, and began to speak with other tongues, as the Spirit gave them utterance." This event marked the beginning of the disciples' bold preaching of the Gospel.

Peter stood up and addressed the crowd, explaining that the outpouring of the Holy Spirit was the fulfillment of prophecy. He spoke boldly about Jesus, whom the crowd had crucified, declaring Him as both Lord and Christ. Acts 2:22-24 records Peter's words: "Ye men of Israel, hear these words; Jesus of Nazareth, a man approved of God among you by miracles and wonders and signs, which God did by him in the midst of you, as ye yourselves also know: Him, being delivered by the determinate counsel and foreknowledge of God, ye have taken, and by wicked hands have crucified and slain: Whom God hath raised up, having loosed the pains of death: because it was not possible that he should be holden of it."

Peter's message was direct and convicting, but it was also filled with hope. He called the people to repentance and offered them forgiveness through Jesus Christ. Acts 2:37-38 says, "Now when they heard this, they were pricked in their heart, and said unto Peter and to the rest of the apostles, Men and brethren, what shall we do? Then Peter said unto them, Repent, and be baptized every one of you in the name of Jesus Christ for the remission of sins, and ye shall receive the gift of the Holy Ghost." Peter extended forgiveness to those who had rejected and mocked Jesus, offering them a second chance through repentance and faith in Christ.

This moment is a powerful example of how we, as Christians, should respond to those who reject or mock our faith. Instead of holding grudges or seeking revenge, we should follow Peter's example and offer forgiveness and the message of hope. Jesus Himself taught the importance of forgiveness in Matthew 6:14-15: "For if ye forgive men their trespasses, your heavenly Father will also forgive you: But if ye forgive not men their trespasses, neither will your Father forgive your trespasses." Forgiveness is not just a suggestion; it is a commandment that reflects the heart of God.

Peter's willingness to forgive and offer a second chance is also seen in his relationship with Jesus. After Peter denied Jesus three times, he was filled with guilt and shame. But after His resurrection, Jesus appeared to Peter and restored him. In John 21:15-17, Jesus asked Peter three times if he loved Him, and each time Peter affirmed his love. Jesus responded by giving Peter the charge to feed His sheep, symbolizing Peter's restoration and second chance to fulfill his calling. This restoration gave Peter the strength and courage to extend the same forgiveness to others.

The early church faced significant persecution, yet they continued to preach the Gospel boldly. Peter and John healed a lame man in Acts 3, and when questioned by the religious leaders, Peter boldly proclaimed

Jesus as the source of their power. Acts 4:10-12 records Peter's words: "Be it known unto you all, and to all the people of Israel, that by the name of Jesus Christ of Nazareth, whom ye crucified, whom God raised from the dead, even by him doth this man stand here before you whole. This is the stone which was set at nought of you builders, which is become the head of the corner. Neither is there salvation in any other: for there is none other name under heaven given among men, whereby we must be saved."

Despite being threatened and commanded not to speak in Jesus' name, Peter and the other apostles continued to preach. Acts 5:29 says, "Then Peter and the other apostles answered and said, We ought to obey God rather than men." Their commitment to sharing the message of repentance and salvation, even in the face of persecution, is a powerful example for us today. We are called to share the Gospel with boldness and compassion, offering forgiveness and hope to those who reject or mock our faith.

Peter's message of repentance and hope was not limited to the Jews. In Acts 10, God directed Peter to share the Gospel with Cornelius, a Gentile centurion. This was a significant moment, as it showed that the message of salvation was for all people, not just the Jews. Acts 10:34-35 records Peter's realization: "Then Peter opened his mouth, and said, Of a truth I perceive that God is no respecter of persons: But in every nation he that feareth him, and worketh righteousness, is accepted with him." This inclusiveness underscores the universality of the Gospel and our call to extend forgiveness and hope to everyone.

Peter's life also shows the importance of humility and reliance on God's grace. Despite his boldness, Peter knew his limitations and relied on the Holy Spirit's power. In Acts 4:13, it says, "Now when they saw the boldness of Peter and John, and perceived that they were unlearned and ignorant men, they marvelled; and they took knowledge of them, that they had been with Jesus." It was clear that Peter's strength came from his relationship with Jesus and the empowering presence of the Holy Spirit.

As we extend forgiveness and share the message of repentance and hope, we must remember that our ability to do so comes from God. Philippians 4:13 reminds us, "I can do all things through Christ which strengtheneth me." We are called to forgive and offer second chances, but it is through Christ's strength and grace that we can fulfill this calling.

Peter's example also teaches us about perseverance in the face of rejection and opposition. In 1 Peter 3:15, he advises, "But sanctify the Lord God in your hearts: and be ready always to give an answer to every man that asketh you a reason of the hope that is in you with meekness and fear." We must be prepared to share our faith and the hope we have in Christ, even when it is difficult. By extending forgiveness and sharing the Gospel, we reflect Christ's love and offer others the opportunity to experience His grace.

In conclusion, Peter's example of offering forgiveness and a second chance to those who crucified Jesus teaches us about the power of grace and redemption. As Christians, we are called to extend forgiveness to those who reject or mock our faith and to share the message of repentance and hope in Christ. Peter's story reminds us that forgiveness is a commandment that reflects the heart of God and that our ability to forgive comes from our relationship with Jesus and the empowering presence of the Holy Spirit. Let us follow Peter's example, offering second chances and sharing the Gospel with boldness and compassion, trusting in God's grace and strength to fulfill our calling. Through forgiveness and the message of hope, we can make a profound impact on the lives of those around us, reflecting Christ's love and extending His grace to all.

Chapter 7 The Support Of Forgiveness

Paul is one of the most influential figures in the New Testament, known for his missionary journeys and profound teachings. One significant aspect of Paul's life was his willingness to forgive and support others, even after they had let him down. A key example of this is Paul's relationship with John Mark. During their first missionary journey, John Mark, who had been traveling with Paul and Barnabas, abandoned them in Pamphylia. This incident is briefly mentioned in Acts 13:13, "Now when Paul and his company loosed from Paphos, they came to Perga in Pamphylia: and John departing from them returned to Jerusalem." John Mark's departure evidently upset Paul, and it later became a point of contention between Paul and Barnabas.

When planning their second missionary journey, Barnabas wanted to take John Mark along again, but Paul strongly disagreed. Acts 15:37-40 recounts, "And Barnabas determined to take with them John, whose surname was Mark. But Paul thought not good to take him with them, who departed from them from Pamphylia, and went not with them to the work. And the contention was so sharp between them, that they departed asunder one from the other: and so Barnabas took Mark, and sailed unto Cyprus; and Paul chose Silas, and departed, being recommended by the brethren unto the grace of God." This disagreement led to Paul and Barnabas parting ways, with Barnabas taking John Mark and Paul choosing Silas as his companion.

Despite this initial conflict, Paul's perspective on John Mark changed over time. In Paul's later letters, we see evidence of reconciliation and support for John Mark. In Colossians 4:10, Paul writes, "Aristarchus my fellowprisoner saluteth you, and Marcus, sister's son to Barnabas, (touching whom ye received commandments: if he come unto you, receive him;)" indicating that Paul had accepted John Mark and saw him as a valuable companion. Furthermore, in 2 Timothy 4:11, Paul specifically asks for John Mark's presence, saying, "Only Luke is with me.

Take Mark, and bring him with thee: for he is profitable to me for the ministry." This statement shows that Paul not only forgave John Mark but also recognized his growth and usefulness in ministry.

Paul's willingness to give John Mark a second chance teaches us a valuable lesson about forgiveness and support. It reminds us that people can grow and change, and we should be willing to offer them opportunities to prove themselves anew. This principle is rooted in the teachings of Jesus, who emphasized forgiveness and reconciliation. In Matthew 18:21-22, Peter asked Jesus, "Lord, how oft shall my brother sin against me, and I forgive him? till seven times?" Jesus replied, "I say not unto thee, Until seven times: but, Until seventy times seven." This passage underscores the importance of limitless forgiveness, reflecting the boundless grace that God extends to us.

Forgiveness and support are crucial aspects of Christian love and community. Ephesians 4:31-32 instructs us, "Let all bitterness, and wrath, and anger, and clamour, and evil speaking, be put away from you, with all malice: And be ye kind one to another, tenderhearted, forgiving one another, even as God for Christ's sake hath forgiven you." By forgiving others and supporting their growth, we mirror the forgiveness and support we receive from God. Paul exemplified this in his relationship with John Mark, showing that even when someone fails us, we should not write them off but instead give them another chance to grow and contribute positively.

Paul's journey of forgiveness and support towards John Mark also illustrates the importance of patience and grace in leadership. Leaders in the church and other areas of life are often faced with situations where their team members or followers make mistakes or fail to meet expectations. Paul's initial disappointment with John Mark did not lead to a permanent rift. Instead, over time, Paul saw John Mark's potential and value, choosing to support him rather than hold a grudge. This reflects the wisdom found in Galatians 6:1, "Brethren, if a man be overtaken in a fault, ye which are spiritual, restore such an one in the spirit of meekness; considering thyself, lest thou also be tempted." Restoration and support should be our goals when dealing with others' shortcomings.

The transformation in Paul's attitude toward John Mark also highlights the transformative power of God's grace in our relationships. It encourages us to believe in the possibility of change and growth in others, just as God continually works to transform us. Philippians 1:6 provides this assurance, "Being confident of this very thing, that he which hath begun a good work in you will perform it until the day of Jesus Christ." Our willingness to forgive and support others plays a role in their spiritual growth and development.

In addition, the Bible calls us to live in harmony and unity, supporting one another in love. Colossians 3:12-14 teaches, "Put on therefore, as the elect of God, holy and beloved, bowels of mercies, kindness, humbleness of mind, meekness, longsuffering; Forbearing one another, and forgiving one another, if any man have a quarrel against any: even as Christ forgave you, so also do ye. And above all these things put on charity, which is the bond of perfectness." By embodying these virtues, we create a supportive and forgiving community where everyone can thrive and grow.

Paul's letters often emphasize the importance of mutual support and encouragement within the Christian community. In 1 Thessalonians 5:11, he writes, "Wherefore comfort yourselves together, and edify one another, even as also ye do." Supporting each other through forgiveness and encouragement helps to build a strong, united body of believers. This principle is also evident in Hebrews 10:24-25, "And let us consider one another to provoke unto love and to good works: Not forsaking the assembling of ourselves together, as the manner of some is; but exhorting one another: and so much the more, as ye see the day approaching." Our gatherings and interactions should be filled with mutual support, forgiveness, and encouragement.

Moreover, Paul's life and teachings remind us that forgiveness is a crucial element of our spiritual health and well-being. Holding onto grudges and refusing to forgive can hinder our relationship with God and others. In Mark 11:25, Jesus says, "And when ye stand praying, forgive, if ye have ought against any: that your Father also which is in heaven may forgive you your trespasses." Forgiveness is essential for maintaining a clear conscience and a healthy, vibrant faith.

The relationship between Paul and John Mark is also a testament to the importance of mentorship and discipleship in the Christian life. By giving John Mark a second chance and supporting his growth, Paul was investing in the next generation of leaders. This principle is reflected in 2 Timothy 2:2, "And the things that thou hast heard of me among many witnesses, the same commit thou to faithful men, who shall be able to teach others also." Mentoring and supporting others in their spiritual journey ensures the continued growth and strength of the church.

Furthermore, Paul's willingness to reconcile with John Mark underscores the importance of humility in our relationships. Recognizing that we all make mistakes and need forgiveness helps us to extend grace to others. James 4:10 advises, "Humble yourselves in the sight of the Lord, and he shall lift you up." Humility allows us to forgive and support others, acknowledging our own need for God's grace and forgiveness.

In conclusion, Paul's example of forgiving John Mark and offering him support after he had abandoned their mission is a powerful lesson in extending second chances. As Christians, we are called to forgive those who fail or disappoint us, recognizing that everyone has the potential for growth and change. By embodying forgiveness, support, and encouragement, we reflect the love and grace of God, building a strong and united community of believers. Let us follow Paul's example, offering second chances and supporting one another in our spiritual journeys, trusting in God's transformative power to bring about growth and change in each of our lives. Through forgiveness and support, we can make a lasting impact on those around us, fostering an environment where everyone can thrive and fulfill their God-given potential.

Chapter 8 The Strength Of Forgiveness

Barnabas is a significant figure in the New Testament, known for his role in the early Christian church and his example of strength in advocating for others. One of the most notable examples of Barnabas's strength is when he forgave Paul, who was then called Saul, for his past persecution of Christians and vouched for him to the apostles. This story highlights the importance of advocating for those who have changed their ways and supporting and encouraging new believers or those returning to faith.

Saul, later known as Paul, was initially a fierce persecutor of Christians. In Acts 8:3, it is written, "As for Saul, he made havock of the church, entering into every house, and haling men and women committed them to prison." Saul's actions caused great fear among the early Christians. However, Saul's life changed dramatically after he encountered Jesus on the road to Damascus. Acts 9:3-6 describes this encounter: "And as he journeyed, he came near Damascus: and suddenly there shined round about him a light from heaven: And he fell to the earth, and heard a voice saying unto him, Saul, Saul, why persecutest thou me? And he said, Who art thou, Lord? And the Lord said, I am Jesus whom thou persecutest: it is hard for thee to kick against the pricks. And he trembling and astonished said, Lord, what wilt thou have me to do? And the Lord said unto him, Arise, and go into the city, and it shall be told thee what thou must do."

After this life-changing encounter, Saul was blind for three days until Ananias, a disciple, was instructed by the Lord to go to him. Ananias was initially hesitant because of Saul's reputation, but he obeyed. Acts 9:17-18 says, "And Ananias went his way, and entered into the house; and putting his hands on him said, Brother Saul, the Lord, even Jesus, that appeared unto thee in the way as thou camest, hath sent me, that thou mightest receive thy sight, and be filled with the Holy Ghost. And immediately there fell from his eyes as it had been scales: and he received sight forthwith, and arose, and was baptized."

Saul's transformation was remarkable, but when he attempted to join the disciples in Jerusalem, they were afraid of him and doubted his conversion. Acts 9:26 records, "And when Saul was come to Jerusalem, he assayed to join himself to the disciples: but they were all afraid of him, and believed not that he was a disciple." It was Barnabas who stepped in to support Saul. Acts 9:27 states, "But Barnabas took him, and brought him to the apostles, and declared unto them how he had seen the Lord in the way, and that he had spoken to him, and how he had preached boldly at Damascus in the name of Jesus." Barnabas's actions required strength and courage. He not only forgave Saul for his past actions but also vouched for him, risking his own reputation to advocate for someone who had genuinely changed.

Barnabas's strength in advocating for Saul is a powerful lesson for us today. It shows the importance of giving people a second chance and supporting those who have turned their lives around. Jesus taught about the importance of forgiveness and reconciliation. In Matthew 6:14-15, He said, "For if ye forgive men their trespasses, your heavenly Father will also forgive you: But if ye forgive not men their trespasses, neither will your Father forgive your trespasses." Forgiving others and advocating for their new beginnings is a reflection of the grace and mercy we receive from God.

Barnabas's example also teaches us the importance of encouragement in the Christian faith. He was known as the "son of consolation" (Acts 4:36), a name that reflects his role as an encourager. Throughout the New Testament, we see Barnabas encouraging and supporting new believers. For instance, in Acts 11:22-24, when news of the new believers in Antioch reached the church in Jerusalem, they sent Barnabas to encourage them. "Then tidings of these things came unto the ears of the church which was in Jerusalem: and they sent forth Barnabas, that he should go as far as Antioch. Who, when he came, and had seen the grace of God, was glad, and exhorted them all, that with purpose of heart they would cleave unto the Lord. For he was a good man, and full of the Holy Ghost and of faith: and much people was added unto the Lord."

Barnabas's ability to see the potential in others and to encourage them is a vital quality for all Christians. Hebrews 10:24-25 encourages us to do the same: "And let us consider one another to provoke unto love and to good works: Not forsaking the assembling of ourselves together, as the manner of some is; but exhorting one another: and so much the more, as ye see the day approaching." Encouraging one another helps to build a strong and supportive community of believers.

Barnabas also played a crucial role in Paul's early ministry. After vouching for him, Barnabas and Paul were sent on a missionary journey together by the Holy Spirit. Acts 13:2-3 says, "As they ministered to the Lord, and fasted, the Holy Ghost said, Separate me Barnabas and Saul for the work whereunto I have called them. And when they had fasted and prayed, and laid their hands on them, they sent them away." Barnabas's support and partnership with Paul helped to spread the Gospel to many regions and establish new churches.

Despite their close partnership, Barnabas and Paul had a sharp disagreement over John Mark, who had deserted them during their first missionary journey. Barnabas wanted to give John Mark a second chance, but Paul disagreed. Acts 15:37-39 records, "And Barnabas determined to take with them John, whose surname was Mark. But Paul thought not good to take him with them, who departed from them from Pamphylia, and went not with them to the work. And the contention was so sharp between them, that they departed asunder one from the other: and so Barnabas took Mark, and sailed unto Cyprus." This incident shows that even strong leaders like Paul and Barnabas can have disagreements, but it also highlights Barnabas's consistent commitment to supporting those who needed a second chance.

Barnabas's support for John Mark was not in vain. Later, Paul recognized John Mark's value in ministry. In 2 Timothy 4:11, Paul wrote,

"Only Luke is with me. Take Mark, and bring him with thee: for he is profitable to me for the ministry." This acknowledgment shows that Barnabas's encouragement and support helped John Mark to grow and become a valuable member of the ministry.

The example of Barnabas teaches us that advocating for others and supporting new believers is crucial in the Christian faith. It requires strength, courage, and a heart full of grace and forgiveness. Galatians 6:1-2 advises, "Brethren, if a man be overtaken in a fault, ye which are spiritual, restore such an one in the spirit of meekness; considering thyself, lest thou also be tempted. Bear ye one another's burdens, and so fulfil the law of Christ." By supporting and encouraging each other, we fulfill Christ's command to love one another and help each other grow in faith.

Barnabas's life also exemplifies the importance of mentorship in the church. He mentored Paul and later John Mark, helping them to develop their gifts and fulfill their callings. Paul also emphasized the importance of mentorship in 2 Timothy 2:2, "And the things that thou hast heard of me among many witnesses, the same commit thou to faithful men, who shall be able to teach others also." Mentoring others in their faith journey helps to ensure the growth and continuity of the church.

Moreover, Barnabas's willingness to forgive and support others reflects the transformative power of the Gospel. It shows that no matter one's past, there is hope for change and redemption through Christ. 2 Corinthians 5:17 declares, "Therefore if any man be in Christ, he is a new creature: old things are passed away; behold, all things are become new." Believing in this transformative power encourages us to support others as they seek to live out their new life in Christ.

In conclusion, Barnabas's example of strength in forgiving Paul and advocating for him teaches us about the importance of supporting and encouraging those who have changed their ways. As Christians, we are called to forgive, support, and encourage new believers and those returning to faith, just as Barnabas did. By doing so, we reflect the grace and mercy of God, build a strong community of believers, and help each other grow in faith. Let us follow Barnabas's example, advocating for and supporting one another with strength, courage, and grace, trusting in the transformative power of the Gospel to bring about growth and change in each of our lives. Through forgiveness and encouragement, we can make a significant impact on those around us, fostering an environment where everyone can thrive and fulfill their God-given potential.

Chapter 9 The Steadfastness of Forgiveness

Jacob, one of the patriarchs of the Bible, is a figure known for his perseverance and steadfast faith in God, especially in the face of repeated deceit by his uncle Laban. Jacob's life story, particularly his interactions with Laban, provides a powerful lesson on patience and forgiveness towards those who repeatedly wrong us, and trusting that God can work through difficult relationships. Jacob's story begins in Genesis, where we learn about his complicated family dynamics and his eventual flight to his uncle Laban's household. After deceiving his brother Esau out of his birthright and blessing, Jacob fled to Laban to escape Esau's wrath. Genesis 28:1-2 says, "And Isaac called Jacob, and blessed him, and charged him, and said unto him, Thou shalt not take a wife of the daughters of Canaan. Arise, go to Padanaram, to the house of Bethuel thy mother's father; and take thee a wife from thence of the daughters of Laban thy mother's brother." Upon arriving, Jacob fell in love with Rachel, Laban's daughter, and agreed to work for Laban for seven years in exchange for Rachel's hand in marriage. Genesis 29:18-20 recounts, "And Jacob loved Rachel; and said, I will serve thee seven years for Rachel thy younger daughter. And Laban said, It is better that I give her to thee, than that I should give her to another man: abide with me. And Jacob served seven years for Rachel; and they seemed unto him but a few days, for the love he had to her."

However, Laban deceived Jacob by substituting his elder daughter Leah for Rachel on the wedding night. Jacob only discovered the deception the next morning. Genesis 29:25 states, "And it came to pass, that in the morning, behold, it was Leah: and he said to Laban, What is this thou hast done unto me? did not I serve with thee for Rachel? wherefore then hast thou beguiled me?" Laban justified his actions by citing local custom and offered Rachel to Jacob in exchange for another seven years of labor. Genesis 29:26-28 explains, "And Laban said, It must not be so done in our country, to give the younger before the firstborn. Fulfil her week, and we will give thee this also for the service which thou shalt serve with me yet seven other years. And Jacob did so, and fulfilled her week: and he gave him Rachel his daughter to wife also."

Despite this deceit, Jacob remained steadfast and served the additional seven years for Rachel. This act of patience and dedication highlights Jacob's perseverance. But Laban's deceit did not end there. He continued to change Jacob's wages multiple times, trying to gain the upper hand. Genesis 31:7 reveals Jacob's frustrations: "And your father hath deceived me, and changed my wages ten times; but God suffered him not to hurt me." Despite Laban's continued deceit, Jacob trusted in God's protection and provision.

Jacob's steadfast faith is evident when God instructed him to return to his homeland. Genesis 31:3 states, "And the LORD said unto Jacob, Return unto the land of thy fathers, and to thy kindred; and I will be with thee." Jacob obeyed God's command, taking his family and livestock and leaving without informing Laban. When Laban pursued and confronted Jacob, God intervened, warning Laban in a dream not to harm Jacob. Genesis 31:24 says, "And God came to Laban the Syrian in a dream by night, and said unto him, Take heed that thou speak not to Jacob either good or bad."

When they finally met, Jacob confronted Laban about his deceitful behavior. Genesis 31:38-42 records Jacob's words, "This twenty years have I been with thee; thy ewes and thy she goats have not cast their young, and the rams of thy flock have I not eaten. That which was torn of beasts I brought not unto thee; I bare the loss of it; of my hand didst thou require it, whether stolen by day, or stolen by night. Thus I was; in the day the drought consumed me, and the frost by night; and my sleep departed from mine eyes. Thus have I been twenty years in thy house; I served thee fourteen years for thy two daughters, and six years for thy cattle: and thou hast changed my wages ten times. Except the God of my father, the God of Abraham, and the fear of Isaac, had been with me, surely thou hadst sent me away now empty. God hath seen mine affliction and the labour of my hands, and rebuked thee yesternight."

Despite Laban's repeated wrongs, Jacob chose to forgive him and made a covenant with him to ensure peace between their families. Genesis 31:44 says, "Now therefore come thou, let us make a covenant, I and thou; and let it be for a witness between me and thee." This act of forgiveness and reconciliation highlights Jacob's steadfast character and his trust in God's plan.

Jacob's story teaches us the importance of showing patience and forgiveness towards those who wrong us repeatedly. Ephesians 4:31-32 instructs us, "Let all bitterness, and wrath, and anger, and clamour, and evil speaking, be put away from you, with all malice: And be ye kind one to another, tenderhearted, forgiving one another, even as God for Christ's sake hath forgiven you." Forgiveness is a crucial aspect of the Christian faith, reflecting the grace and mercy that God extends to us.

Moreover, Jacob's patience and perseverance demonstrate the importance of trusting God in difficult relationships. Romans 12:19 advises, "Dearly beloved, avenge not yourselves, but rather give place unto wrath: for it is written, Vengeance is mine; I will repay, saith the Lord." Instead of seeking revenge, we are called to trust that God will bring justice in His own time and way.

Jacob's steadfastness also highlights the importance of obedience to God's commands, even when facing challenges. His return to his homeland despite potential dangers shows his trust in God's promises. Hebrews 11:8 reminds us of the faith required to obey God: "By faith Abraham, when he was called to go out into a place which he should after receive for an inheritance, obeyed; and he went out, not knowing whither he went." Jacob's obedience, like Abraham's, was rooted in his faith in God's faithfulness.

Additionally, Jacob's willingness to reconcile with Laban teaches us about the importance of seeking peace in our relationships. Romans 12:18 says, "If it be possible, as much as lieth in you, live peaceably with all men." Jacob's covenant with Laban ensured that their families would live in peace, demonstrating the value of reconciliation.

Jacob's story also encourages us to remain steadfast in our faith and trust in God's provision, even when facing deceit and hardship. Philippians 4:6-7 advises, "Be careful for nothing; but in every thing by prayer and supplication with thanksgiving let your requests be made known unto God. And the peace of God, which passeth all understanding, shall keep your hearts and minds through Christ Jesus." Jacob's life exemplifies the peace that comes from trusting God despite difficult circumstances.

Furthermore, Jacob's experiences show that God can use challenging relationships to fulfill His purposes. Despite Laban's deceit, God blessed Jacob and multiplied his wealth and family. Genesis 30:43 states, "And the man increased exceedingly, and had much cattle, and maidservants, and menservants, and camels, and asses." This teaches us that God can bring good out of challenging situations, as Romans 8:28 assures us, "And we know that all things work together for good to them that love God, to them who are the called according to his purpose."

In conclusion, Jacob's story of steadfastness and forgiveness towards Laban provides a powerful lesson for us. We are called to show patience and forgiveness towards those who repeatedly wrong us, trusting that God can work through difficult relationships. Jacob's perseverance, faith, and willingness to reconcile highlight the importance of forgiveness, obedience, and trust in God's provision and justice. By following Jacob's example, we can navigate challenging relationships with grace and faith, knowing that God is at work in our lives, even in the midst of difficulties. Let us strive to embody these principles in our relationships, reflecting the steadfast love and forgiveness that God extends to us, and trusting that He can bring good out of even the most challenging situations. Through patience, forgiveness, and trust in God's plan, we can experience His peace and provision, just as Jacob did.

Chapter 10 The Sacrifice Of Forgiveness

Hosea is a significant figure in the Old Testament whose life and actions vividly illustrate the themes of sacrificial love, forgiveness, and restoration. Hosea was a prophet called by God to demonstrate through his own life the steadfast, unconditional love that God has for His people, Israel, despite their unfaithfulness. One of the most poignant aspects of Hosea's life is his relationship with his wife, Gomer, which serves as a powerful example of forgiveness and restoration in the face of betrayal. Hosea's story begins in Hosea 1:2-3, where God commands him to marry a woman of whoredoms to symbolize Israel's unfaithfulness to Him: "The beginning of the word of the LORD by Hosea. And the LORD said to Hosea, Go, take unto thee a wife of whoredoms and children of whoredoms: for the land hath committed great whoredom, departing from the LORD. So he went and took Gomer the daughter of Diblaim; which conceived, and bare him a son." Gomer's unfaithfulness to Hosea represents Israel's spiritual adultery in turning away from God and worshiping other gods. Despite Gomer's infidelity, Hosea's enduring love and commitment to her reflect God's unwavering love for His people.

Gomer's actions caused great pain and humiliation to Hosea, just as Israel's idolatry caused sorrow to God. Yet, Hosea's response to Gomer's betrayal was not one of rejection but of sacrificial love and forgiveness. In Hosea 3:1, God commands Hosea to show love to Gomer again, despite her unfaithfulness: "Then said the LORD unto me, Go yet, love a woman beloved of her friend, yet an adulteress, according to the love of the LORD toward the children of Israel, who look to other gods, and love flagons of wine." Hosea obeys, buying her back from a life of disgrace and taking her home once more. Hosea 3:2-3 recounts, "So I bought her to me for fifteen pieces of silver, and for an homer of barley, and an half homer of barley: And I said unto her, Thou shalt abide for me many days;

thou shalt not play the harlot, and thou shalt not be for another man: so will I also be for thee."

Hosea's willingness to forgive and restore his relationship with Gomer, despite her repeated betrayals, serves as a powerful example of the depth of God's love and forgiveness for His people. It highlights the importance of being willing to forgive and restore relationships, even when betrayal is involved. Ephesians 4:32 encourages us, "And be ye kind one to another, tenderhearted, forgiving one another, even as God for Christ's sake hath forgiven you." Forgiveness is a central theme in the Christian faith, and Hosea's actions remind us that true forgiveness often requires sacrifice and a willingness to restore relationships.

Moreover, Hosea's love for Gomer reflects God's unconditional love for us. Romans 5:8 emphasizes this unconditional love: "But God commendeth his love toward us, in that, while we were yet sinners, Christ died for us." Just as Hosea loved Gomer despite her unfaithfulness, God loves us despite our sins and failures. This kind of love is not based on our worthiness but on God's nature as a loving and forgiving Father. Hosea's story also teaches us about the redemptive power of love. By taking Gomer back and loving her unconditionally, Hosea provided her with an opportunity for redemption and a new start. This mirrors God's redemptive work through Jesus Christ, offering us a chance for new life and restoration. 2 Corinthians 5:17 declares, "Therefore if any man be in Christ, he is a new creature: old things are passed away; behold, all things are become new." Just as Hosea's love transformed Gomer's life, God's love transforms ours.

In addition, Hosea's obedience to God's command, despite the personal cost, exemplifies the sacrificial nature of true love and commitment. Hosea 6:6 reveals God's desire for steadfast love: "For I desired mercy, and not sacrifice; and the knowledge of God more than burnt offerings." Hosea's life demonstrated this steadfast love, going beyond mere duty to reflect God's heart. His actions challenge us to reflect God's unconditional love in our own commitments, even when it is difficult.

Forgiveness and restoration are also themes emphasized by Jesus in the New Testament. In Matthew 18:21-22, Peter asked Jesus how many times he should forgive his brother who sins against him, suggesting seven times as a generous limit. Jesus responded, "I say not unto thee, Until seven times: but, Until seventy times seven." This response highlights the boundless nature of forgiveness that we are called to extend to others, mirroring the forgiveness we receive from God. Hosea's willingness to forgive Gomer time and again echoes this teaching, showing us that true love is patient and long-suffering.

Hosea's story further teaches us about the importance of faithfulness in our relationships. Just as Hosea remained faithful to Gomer despite her unfaithfulness, we are called to remain faithful in our commitments, reflecting God's faithfulness to us. Lamentations 3:22-23 assures us of God's unwavering faithfulness: "It is of the LORD'S mercies that we are not consumed, because his compassions fail not. They are new every morning: great is thy faithfulness." By remaining steadfast in our love and commitments, we honor God and reflect His character to those around us.

The book of Hosea also highlights the consequences of unfaithfulness and the need for repentance. Hosea 14:1-2 calls Israel to return to the Lord: "O Israel, return unto the LORD thy God; for thou hast fallen by thine iniquity. Take with you words, and turn to the LORD: say unto him, Take away all iniquity, and receive us graciously: so will we render the calves of our lips." Just as Israel needed to repent and return to God, we too must recognize our own need for repentance and seek God's forgiveness. Hosea's call for repentance is a reminder that forgiveness and restoration are available to all who turn back to God.

In our own lives, we may face situations where we are betrayed or hurt by those we love. Hosea's example encourages us to respond with forgiveness and a willingness to restore broken relationships. Colossians

3:12-13 instructs us, "Put on therefore, as the elect of God, holy and beloved, bowels of mercies, kindness, humbleness of mind, meekness, longsuffering; Forbearing one another, and forgiving one another, if any man have a quarrel against any: even as Christ forgave you, so also do ye." By embodying these qualities, we reflect God's love and create a culture of grace and reconciliation.

Moreover, Hosea's story reminds us that true love often involves sacrifice. Just as Hosea sacrificed his pride and comfort to take Gomer back, we are called to lay down our own desires for the sake of others. John 15:13 states, "Greater love hath no man than this, that a man lay down his life for his friends." Sacrificial love is the highest form of love, reflecting the love of Christ who gave His life for us. Hosea's actions challenge us to love others sacrificially, even when it is difficult or painful.

Hosea's relationship with Gomer also illustrates the importance of perseverance in love. Despite repeated betrayals, Hosea did not give up on Gomer. This perseverance is a reflection of God's relentless love for us. 1 Corinthians 13:7 describes love as enduring all things: "Beareth all things, believeth all things, hopeth all things, endureth all things." Hosea's steadfast love for Gomer challenges us to persevere in our love for others, trusting that God can bring healing and restoration.

In conclusion, Hosea's story of sacrificial love, forgiveness, and restoration provides a powerful example for us to follow. His willingness to forgive Gomer and take her back, despite her unfaithfulness, reflects the depth of God's love and forgiveness for us. Hosea's life teaches us to be willing to forgive and restore relationships, even when betrayal is involved, and to reflect God's unconditional love in our commitments. By embodying the qualities of patience, faithfulness, and sacrificial love, we can navigate difficult relationships with grace and honor God in our actions. Let us strive to follow Hosea's example, extending forgiveness and love to those who hurt us, and trusting in God's power to transform and restore broken relationships. Through our actions, we can reflect the steadfast love of God and bring healing and hope to those around us, just as Hosea did.

Chapter 11 The Solidarity Of Forgiveness

Philemon is a unique figure in the New Testament, whose story, as told by Paul in the Book of Philemon, illustrates the importance of forgiveness, solidarity, and unity within the Christian community. The central theme of this short letter revolves around Philemon, a Christian leader in Colossae, and his runaway slave Onesimus, who had wronged him. Onesimus had fled from Philemon, possibly after stealing from him, and had met Paul while Paul was imprisoned. Through Paul's ministry, Onesimus converted to Christianity and became a beloved helper to Paul. In his letter, Paul urges Philemon to forgive Onesimus and to receive him not just as a returned slave, but as a brother in Christ, thus promoting the principles of Christian love, unity, and forgiveness.

The story begins with Paul's heartfelt appeal to Philemon. In Philemon 1:4-7, Paul expresses his gratitude and prayers for Philemon, acknowledging his love and faith: "I thank my God, making mention of thee always in my prayers, Hearing of thy love and faith, which thou hast toward the Lord Jesus, and toward all saints; That the communication of thy faith may become effectual by the acknowledging of every good thing which is in you in Christ Jesus. For we have great joy and consolation in thy love, because the bowels of the saints are refreshed by thee, brother." Paul sets the tone by highlighting Philemon's character and his contribution to the faith community, preparing him for the important request that follows.

Paul then advocates for Onesimus, appealing to Philemon's sense of compassion and Christian brotherhood. In Philemon 1:10-12, Paul writes, "I beseech thee for my son Onesimus, whom I have begotten in my bonds: Which in time past was to thee unprofitable, but now profitable to thee and to me: Whom I have sent again: thou therefore receive him, that is, mine own bowels." By referring to Onesimus as his "son" and emphasizing his transformation and newfound value, Paul underscores the deep bond he has formed with Onesimus and the spiritual change that has occurred.

Paul continues to appeal to Philemon's sense of solidarity and forgiveness. In Philemon 1:15-16, he writes, "For perhaps he therefore departed for a season, that thou shouldest receive him for ever; Not now as a servant, but above a servant, a brother beloved, specially to me, but how much more unto thee, both in the flesh, and in the Lord?" Paul urges Philemon to see Onesimus not just as a returning servant, but as a beloved brother in Christ. This shift in perspective from master-servant to brother-brother reflects the transformative power of the Gospel and the new relationships it creates within the Christian community.

To further emphasize his point, Paul offers to take on any debt or wrongdoing committed by Onesimus. In Philemon 1:18-19, Paul states, "If he hath wronged thee, or oweth thee ought, put that on mine account; I Paul have written it with mine own hand, I will repay it: albeit I do not say to thee how thou owest unto me even thine own self besides." By offering to repay any debt, Paul models the sacrificial love and forgiveness that Christ showed on the cross, reminding Philemon of the forgiveness he himself has received.

Paul's letter to Philemon is a powerful call to embrace those who have wronged us when they seek forgiveness, fostering a spirit of unity and brotherhood in Christ. This message is reinforced throughout the New Testament. In Ephesians 4:31-32, believers are encouraged to forgive one another as God forgave them: "Let all bitterness, and wrath, and anger, and clamour, and evil speaking, be put away from you, with all malice: And be ye kind one to another, tenderhearted, forgiving one another, even as God for Christ's sake hath forgiven you." Forgiveness is essential for maintaining unity and peace within the body of Christ.

Moreover, Jesus Himself taught the importance of forgiveness and reconciliation. In Matthew 18:21-22, Peter asked Jesus how many times he should forgive his brother who sins against him, suggesting seven times. Jesus replied, "I say not unto thee, Until seven times: but, Until seventy times seven." This teaching emphasizes the boundless nature of forgiveness that Christians are called to extend to one another, mirroring the infinite mercy of God.

The concept of brotherhood and unity in Christ is also a key theme in Paul's writings. Galatians 3:28 highlights the unity of believers in Christ, stating, "There is neither Jew nor Greek, there is neither bond nor free, there is neither male nor female: for ye are all one in Christ Jesus." This verse underscores that all believers, regardless of their social status or background, are equal and united in Christ. Paul's appeal to Philemon to accept Onesimus as a brother reflects this principle of equality and solidarity in the Christian community.

Furthermore, the principle of restoring relationships and embracing those who have wronged us is rooted in the teachings of Jesus. In Matthew 5:23-24, Jesus instructs, "Therefore if thou bring thy gift to the altar, and there rememberest that thy brother hath ought against thee; Leave there thy gift before the altar, and go thy way; first be reconciled to thy brother, and then come and offer thy gift." Reconciliation is so important that it takes precedence over religious offerings, highlighting the significance of mending relationships and fostering unity.

Paul's willingness to vouch for Onesimus and to take on his debt also reflects the sacrificial love that Christians are called to show one another. In John 15:13, Jesus said, "Greater love hath no man than this, that a man lay down his life for his friends." While Paul did not physically lay down his life, his willingness to assume Onesimus's debt is an act of profound love and solidarity, demonstrating the lengths to which we should go to support and restore one another.

Additionally, the Book of James reinforces the importance of supporting one another within the Christian community. James 5:19-20 states, "Brethren, if any of you do err from the truth, and one convert him; Let him know, that he which converteth the sinner from the error of his way shall save a soul from death, and shall hide a multitude of sins." By helping to restore Onesimus and advocating for his acceptance, Paul exemplifies this principle of guiding and supporting one another towards spiritual growth and redemption.

In conclusion, the story of Philemon, as encouraged by Paul to forgive and welcome back Onesimus, is a profound example of Christian solidarity, forgiveness, and unity. Philemon's willingness to embrace Onesimus as a brother in Christ, despite his past wrongs, reflects the transformative power of the Gospel and the new relationships it creates within the Christian community. By forgiving those who have wronged us and fostering a spirit of unity and brotherhood, we embody the love and mercy that Christ extends to us. Let us strive to follow Philemon's example, embracing one another with forgiveness and support, and building a strong, united community in Christ. Through our actions, we can reflect the unconditional love of God and bring healing and restoration to those around us, just as Paul encouraged Philemon to do for Onesimus.

Chapter 12 The Saviour Of Forgiveness

Jesus, known as the Savior in the Bible, is the ultimate example of forgiveness, demonstrating this profound act of love and mercy even as He was crucified. The story of Jesus' crucifixion is one of immense suffering and sacrifice, but it is also a powerful testimony of God's love and forgiveness. Jesus' ability to forgive those who crucified Him is a lesson for all believers to follow His example by forgiving even the most grievous offenses. This act of forgiveness is not just a suggestion but a commandment that reflects the heart of God and serves as a powerful testimony of His love.

The story of Jesus' crucifixion is detailed in the Gospels, where we see the extent of His suffering and the depth of His love. In Luke 23:33-34, we read about the moment Jesus was crucified: "And when they were come to the place, which is called Calvary, there they crucified him, and the malefactors, one on the right hand, and the other on the left. Then said Jesus, Father, forgive them; for they know not what they do. And they parted his raiment, and cast lots." Even in the midst of His agony, Jesus prayed for those who were executing Him, asking God to forgive them. This act of forgiveness is unparalleled and shows the depth of Jesus' love and mercy.

Jesus' prayer for forgiveness for His crucifiers highlights a central theme of His teachings—the importance of forgiveness. Throughout His ministry, Jesus emphasized forgiving others. In Matthew 6:14-15, He taught, "For if ye forgive men their trespasses, your heavenly Father will also forgive you: But if ye forgive not men their trespasses, neither will your Father forgive your trespasses." This passage underscores that forgiveness is essential for receiving God's forgiveness. Jesus' own actions on the cross illustrate this principle perfectly, demonstrating that forgiveness should be extended even to those who cause us the greatest harm.

Another powerful teaching on forgiveness is found in Matthew 18:21-22. When Peter asked Jesus how many times he should forgive someone who sins against him, suggesting seven times, Jesus replied, "I say not unto thee, Until seven times: but, Until seventy times seven." This response indicates that forgiveness should be limitless, reflecting the boundless nature of God's forgiveness towards us. Jesus' willingness to forgive those who crucified Him is the ultimate demonstration of this teaching, showing that there is no limit to the forgiveness we should extend to others.

The act of forgiveness is also a powerful testimony of God's love and can be a transformative witness to others. In John 13:34-35, Jesus said, "A new commandment I give unto you, That ye love one another; as I have loved you, that ye also love one another. By this shall all men know that ye are my disciples, if ye have love one to another." Forgiveness is a profound expression of love, and when we forgive others, we demonstrate the love of Christ in a tangible way. This love can be a powerful witness to those who do not know God, drawing them towards His grace and mercy.

Furthermore, forgiveness is crucial for our own spiritual well-being. Holding onto bitterness and anger can harm us more than the person who wronged us. In Ephesians 4:31-32, Paul advises believers, "Let all bitterness, and wrath, and anger, and clamour, and evil speaking, be put away from you, with all malice: And be ye kind one to another, tenderhearted, forgiving one another, even as God for Christ's sake hath forgiven you." By forgiving others, we release the burden of anger and bitterness, allowing us to experience God's peace and joy.

Jesus' example of forgiveness also teaches us about the nature of God's love. In Romans 5:8, Paul writes, "But God commendeth his love toward us, in that, while we were yet sinners, Christ died for us." Jesus forgave those who crucified Him, not because they deserved it, but because of His unconditional love. This same love is extended to us, even though we are sinners. Understanding this helps us to forgive others, knowing that we have been forgiven much more by God.

Moreover, Jesus' act of forgiveness on the cross fulfills the prophetic words found in Isaiah 53:12, which say, "Therefore will I divide him a portion with the great, and he shall divide the spoil with the strong; because he hath poured out his soul unto death: and he was numbered with the transgressors; and he bare the sin of many, and made intercession for the transgressors." By asking for forgiveness for His crucifiers, Jesus interceded on their behalf, showcasing His role as the mediator between God and humanity.

In addition to forgiving those who crucified Him, Jesus taught forgiveness in many parables. One notable example is the Parable of the Unforgiving Servant in Matthew 18:23-35. In this parable, a king forgives a servant a massive debt, but the servant then refuses to forgive a fellow servant a small debt. When the king hears of this, he is angered and reinstates the original debt, illustrating that God's forgiveness towards us should inspire us to forgive others. Jesus concludes the parable with a stern warning in Matthew 18:35: "So likewise shall my heavenly Father do also unto you, if ye from your hearts forgive not every one his brother their trespasses."

Forgiveness is also a central theme in the Lord's Prayer, which Jesus taught His disciples. In Matthew 6:12, part of the prayer says, "And forgive us our debts, as we forgive our debtors." This line emphasizes that our request for God's forgiveness is linked to our willingness to forgive others. It reinforces the idea that forgiveness is a reciprocal act that is vital to our relationship with God.

Another significant instance of Jesus teaching about forgiveness is when He forgives the woman caught in adultery. In John 8:10-11, after her accusers leave, Jesus asks her, "Woman, where are those thine accusers? hath no man condemned thee?" She replies, "No man, Lord." And Jesus says, "Neither do I condemn thee: go, and sin no more." Jesus' response demonstrates His mercy and willingness to forgive, while also encouraging repentance and a new beginning.

Jesus' example of forgiveness extends beyond His crucifixion to His interactions with His disciples. After His resurrection, Jesus appeared to His disciples, including Peter, who had denied Him three times. In John 21:15-17, Jesus asks Peter three times if he loves Him, and each time Peter affirms his love. Jesus responds by instructing Peter to "feed my lambs," "tend my sheep," and "feed my sheep." This interaction reinstates Peter and shows Jesus' forgiveness and restoration, highlighting that even when we fail, Jesus is willing to forgive and restore us.

The Apostle Paul also emphasizes the importance of forgiveness in his letters. In Colossians 3:13, he writes, "Forbearing one another, and forgiving one another, if any man have a quarrel against any: even as Christ forgave you, so also do ye." Paul reinforces that our forgiveness of others should mirror Christ's forgiveness of us. This teaching encourages believers to cultivate a forgiving heart, following Jesus' example.

Furthermore, the book of Hebrews underscores Jesus' role as our compassionate high priest who intercedes for us. Hebrews 4:15-16 says, "For we have not an high priest which cannot be touched with the feeling of our infirmities; but was in all points tempted like as we are, yet without sin. Let us therefore come boldly unto the throne of grace, that we may obtain mercy, and find grace to help in time of need." Jesus' empathy and understanding of our weaknesses make His forgiveness even more meaningful, as He forgives us with full knowledge of our struggles.

In conclusion, Jesus' example of forgiveness, especially towards those who crucified Him, is a powerful testament to the depth of God's love and mercy. His willingness to forgive even the most grievous offenses teaches us that forgiveness is not just a suggestion but a commandment that reflects the heart of God. By following Jesus' example and forgiving others, we demonstrate the love of Christ and offer a powerful testimony to the world. Forgiveness is essential for our spiritual well-being, fostering peace, and releasing us from the burden of anger and bitterness. Jesus' teachings and actions emphasize that forgiveness should be limitless and unconditional, mirroring the boundless forgiveness we receive from God. Let us strive to embody Jesus' example of forgiveness in our lives, extending grace and mercy to others, and reflecting the transformative power of God's love. Through forgiveness, we can build stronger relationships, create a more compassionate community, and draw others towards the love and grace of God.

Conclusion

As we reach the conclusion of "The Freedom of Forgiveness," it is clear that the power of forgiveness, as revealed through Scripture, is transformative and liberating. Throughout this book, we have journeyed through the lives of various biblical figures, each of whom experienced the profound freedom that comes from forgiving others, receiving forgiveness, or both. These stories are more than ancient narratives; they are timeless truths that speak directly to the challenges we face in our own lives.

The story of Joseph, who forgave his brothers for selling him into slavery, teaches us that forgiveness is not only an act of mercy but also an act of trust in God's sovereignty. Joseph's ability to forgive came from his understanding that God can use even the most painful circumstances for a greater good. His forgiveness led to the reconciliation of his family and the preservation of a nation. This story reminds us that when we forgive, we allow God to work through us, bringing healing and restoration in ways we might never have imagined.

King David's journey through sin and repentance shows us the freedom that comes from seeking God's forgiveness. Despite his grave sins, David's heart was broken before God, and he earnestly sought forgiveness. Psalm 51 captures his profound sorrow and his desire to be cleansed and restored. David's story teaches us that no matter how far we have fallen, God's grace is sufficient to restore us when we come to Him with a repentant heart. The freedom David found in God's forgiveness enabled him to continue serving God faithfully, leaving a legacy as Israel's greatest king.

The parable of the prodigal son offers a powerful image of forgiveness and grace. The father's willingness to forgive his wayward son and welcome him back with open arms is a reflection of God's boundless love for us. This story illustrates that forgiveness is not just about erasing wrongs but about restoring relationships and celebrating new beginnings. The prodigal son's return reminds us that no matter how far we have strayed, we are never beyond the reach of God's love and forgiveness.

Finally, the ultimate example of forgiveness is found in Jesus Christ. His prayer for those who crucified Him—"Father, forgive them; for they know not what they do" (Luke 23:34)—is the pinnacle of divine forgiveness. Jesus' willingness to forgive, even in the face of unimaginable suffering, offers us the clearest picture of what it means to be truly free. Through His sacrifice on the cross, Jesus made it possible for us to be forgiven of our sins and to extend that same forgiveness to others.

As you reflect on the examples of Joseph, David, the prodigal son, and Jesus, may you be inspired to embrace the freedom that forgiveness brings. Whether you need to forgive someone who has wronged you, seek forgiveness from another, or accept the forgiveness that God offers you, remember that forgiveness is the key to living a life free from the chains of bitterness, guilt, and regret.

"The Freedom of Forgiveness" is not just a book, but a call to action. It invites you to take the next step in your own journey toward forgiveness, knowing that it will lead you to true freedom in Christ. May you carry these lessons with you, allowing the transformative power of forgiveness to shape your relationships, your faith, and your life. In doing so, you will discover that forgiveness is not just a gift you give or receive; it is a pathway to the abundant life that God has promised to all who follow Him.

Don't miss out!

Visit the website below and you can sign up to receive emails whenever Joshua Rhoades publishes a new book. There's no charge and no obligation.

https://books2read.com/r/B-A-AJLBB-SQBYE

Connecting independent readers to independent writers.

Did you love *The Freedom of Forgiveness*? Then you should read *Restoration - Setting The Bone*[1] by Joshua Rhoades!

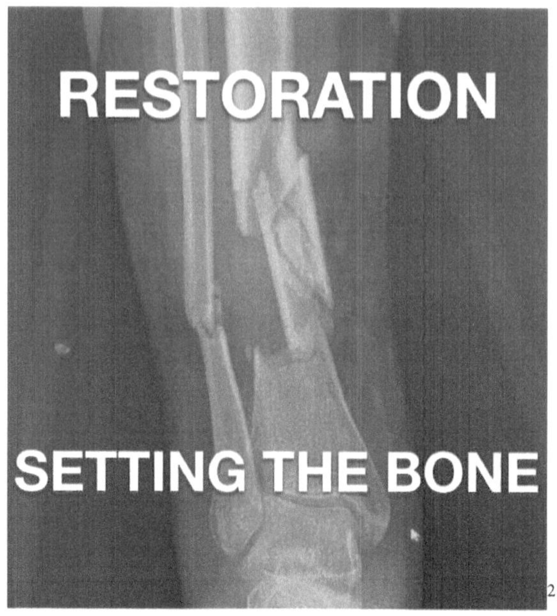

"Restoration - Setting the Bone" dives into the biblical concept of restoration, guiding Christians on their journey to wholeness after experiencing spiritual, emotional, or moral brokenness. Just as a doctor carefully sets a fractured bone to heal properly, God's restoration process involves deliberate actions to realign us with His will, mend our brokenness, and restore us to spiritual health.

The imagery of setting a bone is powerful in describing this process. A broken bone that isn't properly treated can lead to ongoing pain and dysfunction. Similarly, when spiritual fractures—caused by sin, trauma, or life's trials—are ignored, they can result in prolonged spiritual pain

---

1. https://books2read.com/u/3RyQ2p

2. https://books2read.com/u/3RyQ2p

and hinder our ability to fulfill God's purpose. This book serves as a guide for those seeking God's loving and methodical restoration.

The Bible is filled with examples of God's restorative work. From the fall of Adam and Eve to King David's repentance after his sins, Scripture teaches that no matter how broken we are, God is willing and able to restore us. In Psalm 51:10, David's plea, "Create in me a clean heart, O God; and renew a right spirit within me," encapsulates the essence of seeking restoration—recognizing our brokenness and asking God to heal and renew us.

Restoration isn't always quick or easy. Like setting a bone, it can be painful and requires time to heal. It often involves difficult steps such as confession, repentance, forgiveness, and trusting God with the future. Yet, just as a properly set bone becomes strong again, a soul restored by God emerges more resilient and better equipped to fulfill His purpose.

"Restoration: Setting the Bone" walks you through the biblical principles of restoration, offering insights into how God heals our deepest wounds and how we can cooperate with Him in this process. Whether you're seeking restoration for yourself or helping someone else, this book provides the tools and encouragement to embrace God's healing power. It reminds us that no matter how fractured our lives may seem, God is a master at setting the bone, guiding us gently and lovingly toward complete restoration.